Whatever Dude II!

More Meet-ups & Musings

By: Dalia Florea

WHATEVER DUDE II! More Meet-ups & Musings

Published by: Dalia Florea Books

For questions about this book, contact Dalia Florea
www.daliafloreabooks.com[1]
Cover Art by COVER ME - Book Covers
Edited by Kay Phillips

---

1.   http://www.daliafloreabooks.com

Dedication

This book is dedicated to my family, friends, and readers who enjoyed reading *Whatever Dude!*, the first book, and encouraged me to write a second book. To my family and friends, thank you all for lending an ear and sharing a laugh. To my readers, thank you all for giving my book a chance.

A special thanks to my amazing editor, Kay Phillips, who journeyed with me through the foolishness in book one, *Whatever Dude!*

Ladies and gentlemen, I'm back. If you will recall, in *Whatever Dude!* book one, I vowed to give up the idea of online dating for good. I'd planned to meet someone the old-fashioned way.

That idea worked for a while, minus the meeting someone the old-fashioned way part. Bottom line, during my time off the dating site, I. Met. Absolutely. No. One ... nada ... nothing. Not in the supermarkets, not on the metro, not in the mall, not in the coffee house, not in any restaurants, not at events, not at social gatherings, and not even in the park. Okay, I'm lying about the park. I didn't visit any parks, but you get the picture, right? It's not that I was actively looking. I wanted it to be organic.

I don't know if I decided to go back to online dating for dating or the entertainment of it all. I know that sounds wrong to say, but if you read my first book on the subject matter, you'd know why.

Going into this online dating thing for the second round, I felt confident, educated on the dating scene, and ready. I didn't have a laundry list of requirements. They were quite simple, halfway decent looking, a job, not living in his mama's basement, a mouth full of un-stained teeth if you will. A mature man who was honest, trustworthy, and a good communicator. One who re-spected me as a woman.

As I mentioned in my first book, my experiences here are just that, *my* experiences. I'm not an expert in this business and not here to man bash. If you are one of the few good men, then Boo, this is not about you. These dating meet and greets are in no particular order. Some stories are noticeably short, and some are a bit more ex-tended. The names have been changed to protect the – ahem – innocent.

George: The
Friendly Ghost

George worked for a private company as a consultant. He had been stalking me ... um ... attempting to reach out to me when I had been previously on a particular dating site. I never responded to any of his messages because he didn't seem to be my type, and he seemed to be a bit of a stalker. He was always popping in my message mailbox as soon as I signed on—no matter what time of day or night.

It was my first day back on the site, and who pops up in my message box? George. I let his message rest a day or two before I read it. Out of all the messages that

I received in the past two days, he responded to a specific question I included in my profile in which the others paid no attention to. I was darn impressed. Go head George with yo bad self. "Bad," meaning good in this instance. It's an old school term for you youngins. I was so impressed by his answer; I decided to see what Mr. George was all about. We talked a bit via messages on the site before deciding to move the conversation to the phone.

George was interesting and fun to talk with. Here I thought that he was a bug-eyed stalker. For one whole year, I ignored this man's invitations to communicate. Yes, I was on the site for a year, don't judge. How many frogs did the princess have to kiss before she found her prince? It takes time to find a prince. Well, a king in my case.

George invited me to dinner so we could meet face to face to talk. Yes, y'all, dinner. Not a coffee shop or a bench outside of the coffee shop like Mr. Let's Go For Coffee But Too Cheap To Actually Buy Coffee.

My cell phone buzzed just as I was sitting two traffic lights from turning into the restaurant's parking lot. I could see it was George calling. I pushed the button to answer. He was informing me that he was already parked in the lot with his exact location and description of his car. Well, damn. George got a point for being on time. Usually, I was at the meeting spot way ahead of previous prospective dates. Can I say prospective dates? Whatever, you know what I mean.

I parked my car next to his, which was a beautiful Jaguar. I'd previously described my car to him so that he would recognize it when I entered the parking lot. Before I could step out of my car, George was right there to open the door to assist me out. Another point for being a gentleman. Once I got out of the car and was able to take a good look at him, dayam, he was kinda fine. His profile picture did not do him justice. On his profile picture, he seemed to have a big head and beady bug eyes, which immediately brought me back to Devon, the entrepreneur with the long head. Do you remember the one with the long head whose mama kept calling him while we were at breakfast on our first date?

George was shorter than the height I'm usually attracted to, but he was easy on the eyes. Speaking of which, he had beautiful light brown eyes. We hit it off during dinner. We both joked about how it took us a year to go on a date. He was quite humorous, which led me to share a little of my own humor with him.

We ended the date with George asking me out for another date the following day. The next date was to include going out for ice cream, which was how he got date number one. He was the only candidate, for lack of a better word, to pick up on it in my profile.

The following day, we met at a different restaurant for a late lunch. The location was an area I wasn't familiar with, and he was. He wanted to show me around the area before we had lunch. We browsed quaint little shops consisting of home decorations, art, wine, etc. After walking all around and going in and out of the shops, we were both famished. Lunch turned into an early dinner.

The restaurant was crowded; therefore, we took a seat on a bench outside of the restaurant to chat a bit while we waited for our handheld device to signal our table was ready. Again, we had a great conversation with a few humorous moments. The device signaled our table was ready, and we stepped back inside.

During our meal, George took out his phone and started clicking away, taking pictures of me as I was eating. It annoyed the hell out of me, and I asked him to stop. He didn't stop at first, but he finally put his phone down. Had he not, I would have snatched the damn thing away from him. *Is this another weirdo, or is he just going overboard with fooling around?*

After our meal, we walked around the corner to an ice cream shop. We ordered our ice creams and sat outside in the warm summer weather, talking and eating ice cream. George commented that we should go for ice cream at a different place each month. I thought it was a sweet gesture and agreed. It also made me think this guy, in his own sort of way, was committing to continue dating me.

Long after the ice cream had been eaten, it was time to head back. George walked me to my car. As I slid under the steering wheel, he handed me a small envelope and asked that I wait until I got home to open it. As tempted as I was to open it before I got home, I decided to honor his wishes. Another point for being sweet George. Would y'all believe George asked me on another date for the very next day? Three freakin' dates in a row. The entire weekend! Hot damn!

When I arrived home, I pulled out the envelope and opened it. It was a cute little envelope, brown and beige, with a gold seal on the flap that opened. It read, *Dalia, Thank you for an awesome three-day date. The third date tomorrow. I had a wonderful time. George.* I snapped a picture of it to show my girlfriends because I thought it was so sweet.

Our next date was a movie. This time, George wanted me to ride with him in his car. I'm usually not that trusting, but I felt a certain comfort level with him. I didn't want him to know where I lived just yet. Therefore, I requested to meet him at a parking lot, and we'd go from there. He was consistent at being the first to arrive so that I didn't have to wait for him. Y'all already know I'm a stickler for time. In my singing voice, I loved it.

George let me out of my car and walked me to the passenger's side of his car, and waited until I was secured before closing the door. What a gentleman, that George.

On the way to the movies, we were both having fun talking and joking. He then mentioned I sounded like Tiffany Haddish. Come on, George, I wasn't that funny. In fact, most people don't get to see that side of me. I thought it was a little weird how he kept at it.

While waiting for the movie to start, he asked me if I went to the movies often. I told him not often, but if there were something I wanted to see, I would take myself to see it. He replied, "Well, you don't ever have to worry about going to the movies alone again." Hmmm ... it sounded kind of reassuring of another indication that we would be continuing to date. I really liked George. We eased back into our seats with his arm around me as we watched the movie.

By the time we drove back to pick up my car, it was pouring rain. George asked me to stay in the car while he came around to the passenger's side with his large umbrella. Yet another point for dear old George. He held his umbrella over me until I was inside my car.

When I reached home, I texted George to let him know I had arrived safely. He texted back but not with all the hearts and enthusiasm he had been previously displaying.

Monday, there was nothing from George all day. Therefore, I decided to give him a call. He didn't answer. I then texted. He returned my text, but again, not with the *I'm so into you woman* attitude as he'd done on almost every single text or phone call. This went on for another day. He had always been the one to initiate a text or call. I decided to try one last time by sending him a text and asking what was going on. He texted back that he was busy—no word from him the following day or the day after that or the day following that day.

After a three-day weekend date and promises of more movies and ice cream parlor visits, this man had ghosted me! As they say, I should have stuck with my first mind and not given him a chance in hell.

Whatever, dude!

Interrogation
Gary:

G ary worked in the private sector. He didn't reveal much about what he did for a living. Almost as if it was some sort of secret. He wanted to meet at this nice restaurant for our first date. I moved up from the coffee shops, y'all. Not that I don't mind a good cup of coffee, but this second round of men has stepped up their game. At least some of them. Back to Gary. We had previously talked over the phone a few times. We both arrived in the parking lot around the same time. He resembled his pictures. No surprises. He was over six feet and bald. Y'all know I like them tall and bald.

We greeted one another with a light hug and walked into the restaurant. We started with small talk. You know, the weather, traffic, etc. Then, the date turned into an interview session. It was twenty questions back to back: Where do you see yourself in five years? How do you feel about a prenup? What is your take on being in a committed relationship? Have you ever cheated on someone? *Whoa, whoa, whoa, slow your roll, bruh. Can we just get through dinner?* We're nowhere near heading down the aisle into matrimonial bliss. Save some questions for another time. I understood a brother wanting to know our intentions regarding being in a relationship, but prenup questions on the first damn date?

After I was peppered with the first ten questions, I needed a break. I excused myself and headed to the ladies' room. No, I didn't have to pee, surprisingly, since my bladder is normally constant at war with me. I just needed a break from that twenty-question fool to try to come up with a way to end this interview, um, I meant date. I'd wished I was skilled at faking being sick. I never liked attempting to do that because I believed if I did, with my luck, I'd really get sick. Well, it was time to pull up my big girl panties, literally, and go back and face the interrogator.

I returned to my seat and smiled. Before my ass even touched the leather of the seat, he had the nerve to ask me what took me so long, and he was about to come looking for me. Oh, hell, no. He did not just say that. He must have lost his damn mind. At that moment, I said to him, "Listen, I'm not feeling well. I need to go home."

He, in turn, said, "I already paid the check and was going to leave anyway as soon as you got back here." I guess I failed the interview, y'all.

By the time I got inside my apartment, this negro had sent me a text saying that he doesn't think it is going to work out, but he'd like to stay friends if it was okay with me. Um ... that would be a no for me.

Whatever, dude!

Dingy Dennis & the Suspect Brownies:

Dennis was a data analyst and part-time musician. Although he had hair, his hairline was receding, and he was notably losing hair but trying to hold on to it. We met at a restaurant and really hit it off right away. He was funny and made me laugh. We ended up dating for about three whole months. Y'all, three months is a long time in this online dating thing. On several occasions during our telephone conversations, I would ask whether or not we should continue having our profiles on the dating site since it seemed we were now dating exclusively. Dennis always assured me that I was enough for him and said, "There is no need for any other."

Near the end of our third month of dating, Dennis invited me to come over to his home to share a meal. Most of our meals were eating in restaurants because I still had not felt comfortable enough to invite him into my home. However, I did allow him to pick me up for dates, where I would meet him outside. Don't ask; at three months, you would have thought that I would have had him over. I accepted his invitation.

Dennis called me to let me know he was waiting outside to drive me over to his home. He lived in a different part of our metropolitan area than I did. It took us about forty-five minutes to get to his house.

We pulled up to his townhouse, and I could see his two motorcycles he treasured parked out back. He turned the lock to enter the house. We stepped inside. I could not believe what I was seeing. The last time I was shocked beyond belief was when I had mistakenly walked into a men's restroom at the airport and literally saw dicks out. All kinds, black, white, little ones, big ones. Just as I did there, I stood in shock for a few seconds.

We walked from one room into another room. Every room was the same. Dennis was a hoarder. Yes. This. Man. Was. A. Hoarder. He could have easily been on that TV show about hoarders. My stomach turned at the sight of it all. I had a hard time believing he lived this way because Dennis was always well dressed, smelled good, and kept his car spotless, yet he lived the life of a hoarder. Junk everywhere. It appeared whatever he bought, he'd take it out of the box and leave the box/package, or whatever it came in, right there in the room he opened it in. Dishes filled the sink and covered a large part of the countertop, which was also covered with unopened mail. The dining area had no furniture, but it was filled with empty boxes, some music equipment, and stacks upon stacks of unopened mail, some of which were post-dated back two to three years. The space in the living room, where there were two small couches and a TV, seemed to be the only room that was somewhat free of clutter. I mean, there were stacks of mail here and there.

There was no way I was going to have a meal there. He seemed to be a sweet guy, so I offered to at least try and declutter the kitchen countertop. I asked for a pair of rubber gloves and went to work. Dennis promised me that he was going to clear things out, but by the looks of things, that was not going to happen anytime soon. I think he was comfortable with it being just as it was.

While I was moving things around in the kitchen, his doorbell rang. A few seconds later, I heard the voice of a woman. She wanted to know if he had brownies. Wait? What? Why is this woman standing in his living room asking for brownies? He walked back into the kitchen with the woman at his side and introduced her to me. He retrieved the container of brownies from the fridge, took out a few, wrapped them up in foil paper, and walked with her out of the kitchen. When she left, he told me that he liked to help people in the neighborhood with their illnesses. Hmm, what kinda illness does brownies heal? Dude was selling pot and who knew what else. Meanwhile, he professed to be such a holy man.

Oh, by the way, just out of curiosity, but not that it mattered at this point, I thought I might ask him if he still had his profile picture up on that dating site. He responded, "Which one? I have it up on several sites."

Whatever, dude!

Do-Nothing Alfonso aka Mr. "if you act right...":

Alfonso did security at a hospital. After speaking on the phone for several days, he wanted to meet at an IHOP for breakfast. He was kinda cute from his pictures, and I hoped that the meet and greet would turn out fine.

I arrived in the parking lot first. Alfonso phoned to say that he was en route. Shortly after that, a black car pulled up in the parking space next to mine. It was Alfonso. I stepped out of my car. By the time I reached the rear of my car, Alfonso had stepped out of his car. Oh, hell, no! There standing before me was a man who looked as if he'd just rolled out of bed. I kid you not. He was wearing raggedy-ass jeans and a faded, wrinkled sweatshirt. I tried to contain my expression, but I struggled with that. He had the nerve to ask me what was wrong. You are what's wrong, negro!

I wasn't sure if I should get back in my car or what. I took a deep breath and told myself, *Relax, girl, don't be so judgmental. He may have otherwise good qualities. So, let's see if he's a great guy.*

While we waited for our breakfast to come, Alfonso went on about how close he was to his daughters and how no woman would ever be first in his life. He told me a story of a woman who had treated him well, but he had to get rid of her because she wanted to be first in his life. Although I appreciate a man's love and admiration for his daughters, I was ready to move on to another topic. The current one seemed endless. I spoke about some of the things I enjoyed doing and the places I enjoyed going to. I asked Alfonso what were some things he enjoyed. He said that he didn't go anywhere, except to his brother's house to watch sports. He also mentioned he took his younger daughter out to places because his older daughter lived in another state with her mother, his ex-wife. He went on to say how sometimes he would hang out with his younger daughter at her house. She lived with her mother and her mother's husband. He told me that his daughter would sneak him into the house sometimes without permission or knowledge of her mother or her mother's husband. I narrowed my eyes at him. He appeared to be proud of what he'd just revealed, all the while talking with his mouth wide open, chopping down his food. Hmm, we're back on the daughter topic. I injected and asked did he ever go to any concerts or live shows? He, in turn, asked me, "What for?" He said he was comfortable in the comfort of his own home, which Alphonso admitted was his sister's home, where he got into regular fistfights with his adult nephew. Who, by the way, also lived in the home. Then he went on to talk about how he once saw a play on TV that his younger daughter was watching ... blah ... blah ... blah.

"You don't do anything for entertainment?" I asked.

His reply, "I already told you, I don't." He then remembered that he goes to Virginia Beach once a year in December, and if I *acted right,* he would take me.

Whatever, dude!

———— ⟨∾⟩ ————

Here I go again. The dating game was starting to wear me down yet again. I questioned myself as to why on earth was I attempting to do this once more. Hadn't I learned from my previous experiences? Who knows? Maybe deep down inside, I somehow desired more book material as I had already written a book about my previous online dating adventures. After writing that book, a few women who had read it told me that they had met some great guys online. Some said that they remained friends with some of the guys even though the dates didn't work out. A couple of women even said that they had married someone they met online. My eyes sparkled with hope. I decided to hang in there just a little bit longer. Maybe I needed to give it a little more time. Rome wasn't built in a day, right?

Man-Ring Larry:

L arry worked for the federal government. A director in his division, according to him. He was an average looking man and dressed well. We agreed to meet at a Starbucks. We both arrived at the same time. At least, these dates were more on time than the ones I mentioned in my first book. Anywho, I grabbed a table while he ordered us coffee and cheese danishes. I kinda smiled to myself because I reflected on when I couldn't even make it into Starbucks with a previous date. For those who read my first book about online dating, you know who I'm referring to. Yeah, that was Cheapskate Charlie.

Larry brought the coffees and danishes and placed them on the table. We started chatting. He revealed to me that he had met a woman on the dating site, and they met for their first meet and greet at a mall's parking lot. Okay, I was thinking they were going to walk into the mall together. No siree, Bob. He said that she wanted to sit in her car and talk with him because her husband and kids were inside the mall. Damn. That was all. She wanted to know if he would meet her at a hotel from time to time to have sex, and she would tell her husband that she was at work. As he was going on with his story, I happened to glance down at his hand, and dude was wearing a freaking wedding band. I asked, "Are you married?"

This fool told me, "No, it's not a wedding band; it's a man's ring." A man's ring, my butt.

Whatever, dude!

Snippets of messages from my online suitors:

O n two occasions, I received these propositions:

Man #1: "Dinner and $500?" No other words in the message.

Man #2: "$300 and dinner?" Again, no other words in the message.

Hmmm, maybe I should have warned number two that if he were going to continue these shenanigans, he needed to up his offer because another jerk had out bidden him.

———— ⟨∾⟩ ————

"Hey, pretty lady. How are you? Would you mind sending $40 to Cash App so and so? It's for my daughter. She's in college and needs money for food. I can pay you back next week."

Excuse me?

———— ⟨∾⟩ ————

This old dude was in a nursing home. Yes, I kid you not. A nursing home. He had pictures of himself in a wheelchair inside the nursing home. Here's what he said, "Hi, darling. I know that I'm much older than you, but would you be willing to give me a chance? Maybe we can share a cup of coffee or something. What do you think?"

I think the hell not!

———— ⟨∾⟩ ————

"Hey, beautiful. You sure you didn't make a typo on your age? Where do you live? How many bedrooms do you have? Are you looking for a roommate?"

Umm, that's a hard no.

———— ⬦ ————

A pastor asked me if I would be his first lady.

Nah, bruh, not your first or your second. I commit too many sins to be any pastor's first lady. And the church said, "Amen."

———— ⬦ ————

There was even a man who asked if I would marry him and become a mother to his ten-year-old daughter who lost her mother in a car accident.

No can do.

Common Denominator Nicholas:

Nicholas was a doctor. He worked at a hospital and a medical group. He was a tall, handsome gentleman who was a bit older than me. He had a young daughter from one of his previous marriages. Although she did not live with him, he spent time with her when he wasn't working, which didn't leave much room for dating. With both our medical backgrounds, we shared a lot in common and had a lot to talk about.

We met at a diner. I love diners; they're so retro. This one had mini jukeboxes on the table with the music of yesteryears. Nicholas enjoyed talking about his job. But what he enjoyed most of all was talking about how *hateful* his ex-wives were. Oh, oh, here we go. He went on and on. I had literally finished eating breakfast by the time he came to a halt. Out of curiosity, I asked him where he had met his three ex-wives. He met them all at conventions. The lesson here, stay away from those men at conferences. Then, he started complaining about how black women were bitter and blah, blah, blah. If he had taken a look in the mirror, he would have found out exactly who was black and bitter. Doesn't he realize he's the common denominator here?

Whatever, dude!

Jailbird Jason:

J ason, an entrepreneur, was a few years older than me. He was tall, very handsome with a nice body due to working out in a gym daily, sometimes twice a day. He could give some younger men a run for their money with his physique. The first two weeks, we spent a great deal of time on FaceTime, which was Jason's preference. I didn't mind it too much because it allowed me a preview of him before we actually met in person. He had a beard. I'm normally not attracted to men with beards, but his suited him nicely. He was the perfect picture of an older male model and looked fine in whatever he wore—be it casual or dressy.

Our first face-to-face meeting was at a nice restaurant. Jason displayed the behavior of a real gentleman. He was funny and made me laugh a lot. We agreed to continue to see one another and get to know each other better. As it turned out, most of our contact was through FaceTime because Jason would give excuse upon excuse of being super busy with his businesses.

Although we were not spending much time together, Jason seemed to always want to know what I was doing, where I was going, and who I was with, and strangely what I was wearing. There were times that I really didn't feel like Face-timing, but he pressed on to Face-Time. I guess he wanted to see for himself. It was starting to annoy the hell out of me, and I told him so. He also started getting comfortable, exposing his anger toward his ex-wife and calling her names. When I asked that he not do that because it wasn't right since she couldn't defend herself as well as it being disrespectful, he responded, "Why not? She's the biggest bitch that I know." Dude, I'm sure she would have some choice words for you as well.

This damn FaceTime was getting out of control. I remember being at my daughter's house and receiving a call from Jason. He claimed he just wanted to meet her since I had talked about her so much. Right, dude, any excuse to FaceTime to see where I am and who I'm with. Okay, so I decided to FaceTime so that he could meet her. I had already talked to her about him, and this would give her a chance to put a face to a name. He started by chatting with her. After she left the immediate area, this fool asked me to let him see everyone in the room. I hung the damn phone up.

I thought back to the times he had asked me about male friends and the men I worked with. It got me curious about this behavior of his. I had previously done a background check on him, but I needed to dig deeper because I was obviously missing something. I know background checks don't let you know if they're crazy, but I could find out what their cray-cray actions might lead to. Y'all, do them background checks.

Since my previous check did not come up with much, I decided to check the courts in his district to see what I could come up with. His behavior was getting to be a bit controlling for me. Boom! I found out there were not only charges against him from some of his customers, but this man was also a wife-beater! A wife-beater! Okay, I did understand that information is sometimes reported one-sided, but in this instance, there were a few documented domestic violence entries. Major deal breaker! Shit, I wasn't giving this fool the chance to try beating my ass up or me going to prison for killing his ass in the process. It was not worth it. I stopped all contact with this man. He had not attempted to reach out to me, either.

A couple of weeks later, I was sitting in Starbucks with one of my girlfriends, and I got a text from Jason. I didn't know why I hadn't thought of blocking him. I wasn't sure if I wanted to read it because I didn't know if it was a threat or what. He texted: *I think it's that time. Good luck and nice knowing you.*

Negro, please.

Whatever, dude!

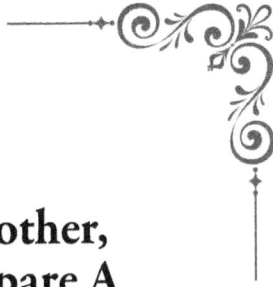

Kevin: Brother, Can You Spare A Mattress?:

Kevin was an average looking fireman with a great sense of humor. We had great conversations over the phone about people and life, in general. Kevin had a twin brother, and he shared many memories of growing up with him. When they were young, they played jokes on each other's girlfriends. He also mentioned that he pretended to be his brother and visited one of his brother's adult ex-girlfriend, and she thought he was his brother. He claimed that it had been years ago. His brother had recently broken off with the woman, and Kevin was

37

single and feeling horny, and thought he would visit the ex-girlfriend. According to him, that dog's visit was successful. I asked did his brother ever find out about it. Kevin claimed that his brother encouraged it. Twin dogs.

We met for the first time at a restaurant. Kevin resembled his profile pictures, which was comforting because I had met a few who came nowhere close to their profile pictures. After meeting, we went on a few more dates.

One day, while on a phone call with Kevin, he told me that he was looking to purchase a mattress for his bed. I asked him where he had been looking and suggested that it would be a good idea if he went to the mattress store in person to get a feel for the mattress before he spent money on one. He didn't quite seem interested in my suggestion. I couldn't understand why not, but, hey, to each his own right?

A couple of days after that call, Kevin told me that he saw a woman on Craigslist selling a mattress. Used, y'all. He said the woman mentioned it had bed bugs, but it had been cleaned and free of them. Ew! I knew this fool was not thinking of buying it. *Who in their right mind would even give a thought to buying somebody's bug-ridden mattress?*

During this conversation, Kevin presented me with a "hypothetical" situation. He said if he had made a deal with someone at one price and the person came back and told him something different, what would I do? Hmmm. I asked him to give me all the specifics to be in a better position to answer the question. He instantly got upset with my response, said he had to go, and hung up on me. Really, dude. Since he had not gone into specifics and was not forthcoming, I could only presume the man who put out fires was in the process of purchasing that bug-ridden mattress he had just told me about. Well, go ahead on and sleep with them bugs, Kevin.

I didn't hear from Kevin again until several days later when I received a text. What is up with the texts? In the text, he said that I was a nice lady, but it wouldn't work out because I lived too far, and he preferred to date someone who lived closer to him.

Whatever, dude!

———————— ⟶ ◦⟨𝒮⟩ ————————

I had finally given up the idea of finding love through online dating. It may have worked for some, but it was not working for me. I deleted all my accounts.

I couple of months later, I was reconnected with a man whom I had dated before. No, he wasn't someone whom I met on an online dating site.

Strange as it may sound, we first met on Twitter. That's right, Twitter. It wasn't a romance thing. We were just Twitter friends. We were tweeting here and there. We discovered that we had much in common. We both loved jazz. In fact, he happens to be a professional saxophonist who plays contemporary jazz. We are both New Yorkers. He's a Brooklyn boy, and I'm a girl from Queens. We shared endless stories about growing up in NYC as kids, teenagers, and young adults.

While I visited a friend in NY, we met one evening at a jazz club and enjoyed each other's company. Our chemistry seemed to have come quickly and naturally.

We had become great friends. Before we knew it, that friendship developed into something more. When we were not in each other's company, we would spend hours at a time over the phone. We never got tired of conversing and always had something to talk about.

Having a long-distance relationship had started to take its toll on us. We began to drift apart until it no longer worked for us. We maintained a friendship; however, contact was far and few.

Although Keyan and I were no longer together, he would run across my mind often, especially whenever I read or saw something we had talked or laughed about. I missed our relationship, but I was stubborn with the thoughts of second chances. I did not believe in trying to rekindle something that didn't work the first time.

Almost four years later, and within a few months of deleting my dating apps, while in my kitchen preparing a meal, my phone rang. I checked the caller ID, which showed the caller was none other than Mr. Keyan Williams.

Keyan is six-six tall and handsome, y'all. Yes, a tall glass of water. He is a talented saxophonist and an Assistant Director of Information Technology at a well-known prestigious college. That's right. Smart and handsome.

We chatted for a while on the phone like old times. We caught up with what was going on in one another's life.

Six months later, he took me to a lovely restaurant for dinner. We had finished dinner and ordered dessert. Halfway through the desert, Keyan rose from his seat and came around to my side of the table and bent to one knee. He said a few words of affirmation to me. For the life of me, I can't remember a word to this day, but they sounded good at that moment. He then pulled out a black velvet box from his pocket, opened it, and asked me to marry him. I stared at the beautiful, sparkling engagement ring and was filled with emotions. All I could muster was, "Oh my, God!" which I repeated about three times, I'm told.

He asked, "Is that a yes?" Poor man, it escaped me that he was still on his knee until I gave him an answer. I nodded my head and said, "Yes."

Keyan Williams and Dalia Florea were married in a private ceremony on August 20, 2020.

Author's Note

Dear Reader,

I hope you enjoyed *Whatever Dude II! More Meet-ups & Musings.* As an author, I love feedback. So, tell me what you liked, what you loved, even what you hated. I'd love to hear from you. You can write to me at daliafloreabooks@gmail.com and visit me on the web at daliafloreabooks.com.

I need to ask a favor. If you're so inclined, I would love a review of Whatever Dude II! More Meet-ups & Musings. Whether you loved it or hated it, I'd just enjoy your feedback.

Reviews can be tough to come by these days. You, the reader, have the power now to make or break a book.

Thank you so much for reading, *Whatever Dude II! More Meet-ups & Musings,* and for spending time with me.

In Gratitude,
Dalia Florea

Dalia grew up in Queens, New York, and now makes her home in Ithaca, New York. She is the author of *Mirrored, Teardrops Know My Name, Reflections,* and *Whatever Dude!* Her debut, *Mirrored,* reached Amazon's Best-

seller's list in Women's Detective Fiction. Her second
novel, *Teardrops Know My Name,* also reached Amazon's
Bestseller's list in African American Mystery, Thriller
and Suspense. *Whatever Dude!* book one also made
Amazon's Bestseller's list. She is an avid reader who enjoys writing fictional stories with a mixture of mystery
and suspense, sprinkled with romance. When she isn't
crafting mystery suspense stories with a dash of romance,
she enjoys reading, sipping coffee, attending live music
concerts, visiting wineries, and solving puzzles.

Visit her at www.daliafloreabooks.com[1]

Twitter and Instagram: @DaliaFlorea

Pinterest: Dalia Florea

---

1.   http://www.daliafloreabooks.com

www.ingramcontent.com/pod-product-compliance
Lightning Source LLC
Chambersburg PA
CBHW022133280326
41933CB00007B/677